CHRIS MAKES FRIENDS

STEPHANIE JEFFS
ILLUSTRATED BY JACQUI THOMAS

Everywhere Joe went,
Christopher Bear went, too.
Joe laughed with Christopher Bear on the swing.
They giggled together as they whizzed
'round and 'round on
the merry-go-round.

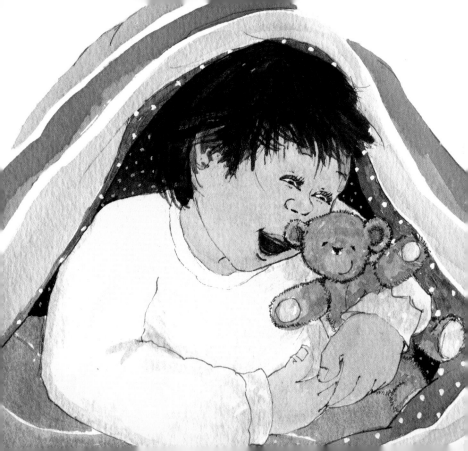

At the end of the day, Joe and Christopher Bear
snuggled under the covers together.
Joe loved being with Christopher Bear.
And he knew that Christopher Bear
loved being with him.
"You're my best friend," Joe whispered.
"My very, very best friend."

But today Joe and Christopher Bear
were going to preschool.
"I want to stay with you," Joe told his mom.
"You'll have a lovely time," said Mom.
She gave Joe a kiss.
"You'll meet some new friends."
Joe held on to Christopher Bear very tightly.
Christopher Bear held on to Joe.

Joe stood and watched.
Everyone was busy.
"Hello, Joe," said Miss Rosie.
"What would you like to do?"

Joe didn't say anything.
So Miss Rosie asked
Christopher Bear,
"What would *you* like to do?"

"Oliver's making breadsticks," said Miss Rosie.
"Come and see."
"Yum, yum," said Oliver.
He pushed his glasses onto his nose,
then he gave Christopher Bear a breadstick.
Joe smiled at Oliver. Oliver smiled back.
Oliver showed Christopher Bear his rabbit.
"This is Flopsy," he said.

"I'm plowing a field," said Ben.
He was pedaling the tractor.
He smiled a huge cheeky smile.

"Do you want to help?" asked Miss Rosie.

Joe wasn't sure.

"Look!" laughed Miss Rosie.

"Christopher Bear knows what to do."

Joe helped Christopher Bear.

He could do it, too!

Later on they went outside.
"Shall I push you?" asked Miss Rosie.
Joe didn't answer.
"Can I swing, too?" asked Elizabeth.
Elizabeth stretched her legs in and out.
Joe stretched his legs, too.
He watched as Elizabeth's braids swung in and out.
"I'm flying!" laughed Joe, soaring high into the air.
"I'm flying, too!" laughed Elizabeth.

Joe ran around the playground.
Everyone else seemed to be running, too!

"Hello, Joe!" said Jessie, rushing past.
"Hello, Joe!" said Ben.
"Hello!" said Joe, chasing them.
They grabbed each other's hands
and whizzed 'round and 'round.
Joe laughed. He felt like a spinning top.

"I'm Harry the builder," said Harry with the digger.
"I'm Builder Joe," said Joe. Together they
piled up the sand.
"I'm digging for treasure," said Oliver.
Just then Jessie came along.
"Let's make a train!" laughed Jessie,
and she held on to Joe's waist.
They all ran off around
the playground again.

"Time to come in," called Miss Rosie.
Joe ran. But then he tripped and fell!
A horrible, sharp sting stabbed his hands
and knees.

Two big, fat tears rolled down his
cheeks and splashed onto
Christopher Bear's fur.

Joe screwed up his eyes.
His knees really hurt.
"Oh Joe," said Jessie, helping him up.
"Miss Rosie!" shouted Elizabeth.
"Here," said Harry,
giving Joe his hanky.
Miss Rosie gave Joe a big hug.

Joe cuddled Christopher Bear,
and Oliver gave him Flopsy
to hold.

At bedtime, Joe snuggled under the covers
with Christopher Bear.
Joe told Mom about everything
that had happened during the day,
about Oliver and Flopsy, and Ben on the tractor,
about Elizabeth's braids swinging up
and down, about Jessie and the train,
and about Harry giving him
his hanky. Joe liked his new friends.

"Shall we say thank you to God
for your friends?" said Mom.
So Joe said, "Thank you, God,
for Oliver and Flopsy,
and for Harry and Jessie who helped.
Thank you for Ben with the cheeky smile,
and Elizabeth with her swinging braids.
Thank you, God, for Miss Rosie,
and for my very best friend, Christopher Bear."
And Christopher Bear just smiled
his crooked smile made
of button thread.

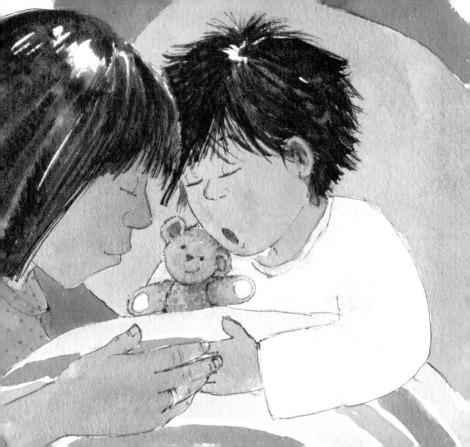

First Augsburg Books edition. Originally published as *Christopher Bear Makes Friends* copyright © 2002 AD Publishing Services Ltd. 1 Churchgates, The Wilderness, Berkhamsted, Herts HP4 2UB

ISBN 0-8066-4401-X
AF 9-4401
First edition 2002

02   03   04   05   06   1   2   3   4   5   6   7   8   9   10